The Railway its bu
want

The Sleaford-Bourne Branch of the Great Northern Railway

Alan Stennett

'Your directors have found it necessary, in protection of your interests, to apply to Parliament for powers to construct lines from Bourne to Sleaford, and from Honington, on the Boston and Sleaford Railway, to Lincoln'.

Great Northern Railway 'Report of the Directors to the 35th half-yearly Ordinary General Meeting of the Proprietors' 20 February 1865

'Application shall be made to the Board of Trade for permission to abandon the ...railway hereinafter specified, namely:-

(1) The Railway authorised by the Great Northern Railway (Sleaford to Bourn) Act 1865

Great Northern Railway Circular to Proprietors 8 February 1868

Dedication

This book is dedicated to the memory of the late Richard 'Dick' Tarpey, without whose research it would not have been possible.

Grateful thanks to Graham Morfoot, Brian Lawrence, Fraser Ross, Roy Harrison, J H Platts, John Bonser, the GNRS, the late Richard Goodman and Rev. David Creasey, and others for the use of photographs and other material

Billingborough station, the largest on the Sleaford to Bourne branch. R Tarpey collection

ISBN 978-0-9574763-1-8

Published by Alan Stennett. Cover design Philip Eldidge

Printed by Allinson Print & Supplies, Allinson House, Fairfield Industrial Estate, Louth, Lincs LN11 0LS

Contents

E1 Class locomotive passing Bourne East signal box with the train from Sleaford.
R Tarpey collection

Before the railway

The south Lincolnshire towns of Bourne and Sleaford, in the Parts of Kesteven, and the string of spring-line villages that follow the fen edge between them, have never lacked for communication opportunities. The road now known as Mareham Lane, from Rippingale to Sleaford, virtually parallel with the later rails, appears to be an extension of King Street, the Roman road from Peterborough to Bourne, which may itself have used an older track between the edge of the higher Lincolnshire Heath and the Fen. Slightly further to the west, the modern A15 through the small market town of Folkingham was one of Lincolnshire's earliest turnpikes, carrying much of the London-Lincoln traffic by way of Peterborough.

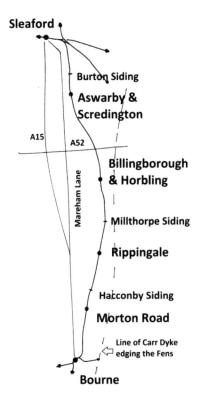

The waterway known as the Carr Dyke, attributed to the Romans, but possibly early medieval, while probably principally a catch-water drain may also have served as a transport water way, as did the River Slea, the Glen and other links towards the sea.

This relatively good communication ability – at least in nineteenth century terms – may have been one of the reasons for the lack of interest shown by railways companies when they began to consider routes through and within the county. The cost of building through the rolling countryside of the Heath was also off-putting to the early surveyors and engineers, although initial plans for north-south routes through the county did include one from Peterborough to Lincoln that would have passed through Sleaford, and two from Cambridge to Lincoln that were intended to serve either Bourne or Folkingham, but not both!

Initial railway connections to the county were provided by coaches serving stations elsewhere, with the earliest recorded direct railway connection being from Lincoln to Denbigh Hall station on the London and Birmingham Railway. T Shaw & Co's 'The Railway', starting in 1838, served Sleaford, Folkingham and Bourne, all with easy links to our patch of the county. The terminus for the coaches moved to Peterborough when that town achieved a railway connection, and although the through coaches to Lincoln ended with the arrival of the railway from Newark in 1846, the southern towns kept their services for some years.

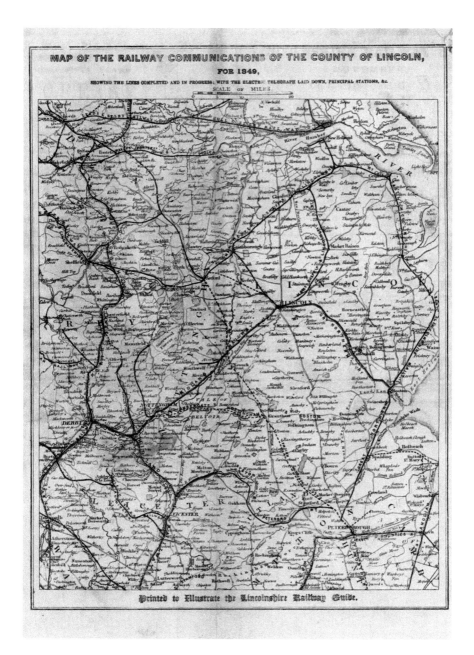

Lincolnshire's Railway Network in 1849. The GNR's line to the north, the modern East Coast Main Line did not open until 1852 and is shown as a dotted line

5

Major railway projects were completed in the county in the late 1840s and early 1850s, but Sleaford, Bourne and the villages were all by-passed during this first phase, with the nearest tracks passing through Spalding and Boston to the east and Grantham to the west. Sleaford achieved railway status in 1857 with the Sleaford, Boston and Midlands Counties Railway, on a route between Grantham and Boston.

GN train leaving Sleaford station. Date not known. Author collection

Bourne was linked to what we now know as the East Coast Main line, first by the Edenham and Little Bytham Railway, a private line constructed in 1856 across his Grimsthorpe Castle estate by Peter, Lord Willoughby de Eresby, and then by the Bourne & Essendine Railway, opened in 1860. The Spalding and Bourne Railway, part of the Midland and Eastern, later incorporated into the Midland and Great Northern Joint, connected it to neighbouring Spalding six years later.

Edenham and Little Bytham locomotive. 'Havilah'
Author collection

Both towns were important market centres for the local villages, although Folkingham drew in some business between the two, but all were close enough to one or other of the towns for a farmer's trap or traders cart to serve them adequately for their business needs.

Politics triumphant and defeated

Ironically, when the railways came to the villages, the driving force behind the plan was more a matter of railway politics than local needs. The Great Northern Railway Company, which dominated the tracks in the south and east of Lincolnshire, had a very lucrative trade in coal from the Yorkshire and East Midlands coalfields to London and the south. The Great Eastern Railway, which had an even more dominant hold on railway services in East Anglia, wanted to gain access to those coalfields in order to serve its own catchment and on to its London termini. In order to achieve that aim, it proposed, or supported, a number of lines through Lincolnshire that joined its own routes in the south to existing companies serving Yorkshire. One such, put to Parliament in 1864, was the Great Eastern Northern Junction Railway running from Cambridge by way of Peterborough to Lincoln, then on to a connection with the Lancashire and Yorkshire Railway near Doncaster, which would have served both Bourne and Sleaford.

To counter such proposals, the Great Northern won Parliamentary permission to build two lines. One ran from Lincoln to the existing tracks between Grantham and Sleaford, with a junction at Honington allowing trains to run direct to either town. The second was from Sleaford to Bourne, by way of the villages between. The political basis for the latter proposal was clear from a statement to the GN Board, in February of 1864 that 'Your directors have felt it necessary, in protection of your interests, to apply to Parliament for permission to construct lines …..from Bourne to Sleaford…'. The line would be constructed 'at no heavy expense'. The Chairman, Col. Packe, MP, added 'We thought the better thing was to construct them ourselves, so that we should not be forced hereafter to purchase them off contractors who might have made them at considerably greater expense'. The minutes note that 'Hear, hear' was recorded from the gathering. It is apparent that the line was never really seen as an alternative to the major freight route proposed by the GE!

The GN plans were accepted by Parliament, and those of the GE turned down, but there was a distinct lack of urgency about the Bourne to Sleaford section. The construction between Lincoln and Honington began almost immediately; with services commencing in April 1867, but very little happened south of Sleaford. The Rutland and Stamford Mercury, reported on a meeting in November 1867 at the Sessions House in Bourne 'to consider how the G.N.Co. might be compelled to build the Sleaford & Bourn line in accordance with the Act already obtained'. The Grantham Journal noted, in February 1867, the imminent start of the services between Grantham and Lincoln, and called for 'tangible proof of the repeated and positive promises' that work would soon start between Sleaford and Bourne.

'When the public were solicited to sign a petition in favour of the Bill, it was promised that a line between the two latter towns would most certainly be made if the company were so

fortunate as to obtain their object. At this season of the year when coals are so much needed by all classes, the coal merchants, well knowing that we cannot help ourselves, increase the price, and when appealed to, at once throw the blame upon the railway company. The price now stands here at 25/- per ton (£1.25), which the poorer classes undoubtedly feel much.'

In response, the GN applied the following year for permission not to build the line.

The reason for this apparent change of heart was that the GN and GE had begun to work together on a joint project that seemed to offer benefits to both parties.

The GE had negotiated running powers – the right to operate their trains over another company's tracks – over GN rails from March to Spalding, and the GN had completed their Lincolnshire Loop Line by extending it from Gainsborough to Doncaster. This avoided a previous diversion, over Manchester, Sheffield and Lincolnshire tracks between Gainsborough and Retford. Building a new, jointly owned section between Spalding and Lincoln would then offer a fast, lightly graded route from Cambridgeshire to Yorkshire. Agreement was still hard to come by - one plan was rejected in 1866 by GE shareholders as being too expensive, and another failed because of complications about running rights held by other companies. A further proposal by the GE to link up with the Lancashire and Yorkshire was again opposed by the GN, who then made several attempts to merge with the GE, which were blocked by the GE directors. Eventually, agreement was reached in 1879, and the GN & GE Joint Railway opened three years later.

The agreement to build the Joint line meant that the GN's need to build from Bourne to Sleaford in order to block the GE no longer existed, and the company applied to be able to end the project. In this case, politics defeated them because of local support for the line.

The government's Board of Trade turned down the GN's application in 1868 and the plans were reluctantly implemented, although the company downgraded from the proposed double track to a single line, as well as persuading the local landowners to accept agricultural value for their land, rather than the development price. In August 1870 eight contractors bid for the contract to build the line with tenders ranging from T B Nelson's £40,298, down to £29,363 quoted by J Firbank who was awarded the contract. S & W Pattinson bid £4,585 to build the station buildings, which was the lowest of three bids, and was accepted. Pattinsons later came back with a claim that they had made a mistake of £328 in their calculations, but the company refused to allow them to change the quotation.

The line was relatively easy to build, running for 17.25 miles, mostly along flat Fen terrain, with the steepest gradient a mere 1 in 120.

It required very little in the way of engineering works, with the exception of a low six-arch viaduct and a fine three-arch bridge between Horbling and Billingborough.

BRIDGE AT 7^m 40^{ch}
Scale 20ft to an inch

The total cost came in at just over £100,000, and it seems Firbanks had more problems with the locals than with the construction.

Three-Arch Bridge on Stow Road, Horbling

'Wm Sutton of Hacconby was charged with stealing two wooden posts, value 8 shillings, the property of Joseph Firbank, contractor for the Bourn and Sleaford Railway, and was sentenced to fourteen days hard labour at Folkingham Goal.' Grantham Journal Aug 1871.

Billingborough would seem to have been the main base during construction. Records show that there were 49 railway employees living there in 1871, with a further 5 in Horbling, including the contractor's agent, a civil engineer, two inspectors, a foreman and an engine driver. The remainder were craftsmen or labourers. Only 11 railway workers lived elsewhere on the route of the line, of which 9 were at Scredington. Others may, of course, have been resident in Bourne or Sleaford.

Such a large gathering of men would have been good for the village's pubs and other traders, but were not an unalloyed benefit, as a report in the Stamford Mercury of October 11 1870 proved.

'On Saturday evening last, between 11 and 12 o'clock, the inhabitants of this village were greatly alarmed by fierce shouts and cries which proceeded from a series of fights between some gipsies and railway navvies..... The former, finding that they were getting the worst of it, made good their escape. The navvies, thinking they had secreted themselves in some vans standing at the south end of the town, repaired thither, and had it not been for the entreaties of some bystanders, the vans would have been overturned. The cries of the women inside were most pitiable.'

There was more trouble in February 1871, when the workmen at Billingborough came out on strike. However, they were persuaded to go back to work, although what the paper described as 'the ringleaders' were sacked.

The locals were also up in arms about the long delay in opening the line. A meeting in Billingborough, also in 1871, demanded that 'the penal clauses in the Act' should be enforced

9

on the company. This would have required the company to pay £5 a day for every day that the line was not completed that was more than five years from the passage of the Act.

The line was finished in 1871, and the first goods trains ran between Sleaford and Billingborough on 10 October. The tracks were inspected for passengers by Lt. Col. C S Hutchinson two months later. The inspector required a connection with a ballast pit near Sleaford to be taken out before the line could come into full operation. He also took account of the promise that 'sheds' for passengers were being provided at Sleaford, Bourne and Billingborough, the largest community between the towns, and the commitment by the connecting companies at each end to provide locomotive turntables in the near future. With those provisos, the line opened throughout on 2 January 1872, and passengers were carried from that date.

The promises to modify the track layout and provide the other essential facilities at Sleaford were carried out, according to the 'Rail' publication in January 1872.

'At Sleaford, the alteration of sidings and signals rendered necessary by the opening of the Bourn line is nearly completed, and the foundations of the engine turntable, being made by Mr. Stirling at Doncaster, are being fixed.'

The Newark Advertiser noted in the same month that the foundations were being laid 'by the company's men', and Rail confirmed in May of that year that the turntable was then in place.

A turntable was also installed at Bourne, where a junction was made with the Midland and Eastern, with an annual payment to the M&E of £25 for the use of 143 yards of their line! The opening of full service on the line was noted by the Mercury three days after the event.

'The new line from Sleaford to Bourn was opened Tuesday (2nd). Five trains each way on weekdays, but none on Sundays. The first train from Sleaford at 6 a.m., the last (to Bourn only) 6-50 p.m. From London, three trains to Sleaford via Essendine daily and three back, Sundays excepted.'

The timetable was revised fairly quickly, with that early train from Sleaford moved to later, and modifications made to the Monday service, with an early train from Bourne added, and the first afternoon train back delayed by twenty minutes. The journey time, including stops at all four stations, was fifty minutes, giving an average speed of around 20 mph, which casts doubt on my grandfather's comment that he could get from Billingborough to either end of the line faster by pony and trap than by train!

The opening seemed to come as a surprise to the villagers of Billingborough, as the local correspondent of the Grantham Journal reported.

'The Opening Day of the Sleaford and Bourn line on Tuesday had for some time been looked forward to, and a public demonstration was intended to be made in honour of the event, but in consequence of the inhabitants not being informed of the fact until late on Saturday evening it was impossible to effect the necessary arrangements. The bells of the parish church, however, sent forth some merry peals throughout the day, and crowds of people assembled at the station to witness the arrival and departure of the trains. The engines were very neatly decorated with flags and evergreens.'

The Bourne and Sleaford Railway was now ready to serve the communities along its route, but not without some early problems at both ends.

'Bourn Correspondant (sic). Sleaford and Bourn Railway. During the short time this line has been open the amount of business done at Billingborough station has far exceeded the expectations of the officials. The manager of the traffic department has however deemed it prudent to make several alterations in the arrival and departure of the trains. On Friday afternoon, on arrival at Bourn of the train from Sleaford, the engine, after taking in water, ran off the rails; but it was got on again in about twenty minutes. It is supposed that the great amount of wet we have had lately occasioned the sleepers to give way.' Grantham Journal 3 February 1872.

'On Monday morning (1st July) the 6.30 train from Sleaford to Bourn was detained for about two hours by an accident near to the distant signal, a short way from the Sleaford station. All the carriages safely passed the points, but for some cause or other the guard's van left the metals, and the train ran about 400 yards before the matter was observed by the driver. Fortunately no serious damage was done, and beyond detention the passengers were not inconvenienced.' Grantham Journal 6 July 1872.

The original stated intention that the line was to be part of a new alternative route from Lincoln through Sleaford to the GN's main line at Essendine was never carried through. There are some indications that the necessary link at Honington to allow through running from the Lincoln to Grantham line to Sleaford and on to Bourne was started, but it was never completed.

OPEN
BOURNE & SLEA

TRAIN S
From 2nd JAN
UNTIL FURTHE

UP.—WEEK DAYS.

	a.m.	a.m.	a.m.	p.m.		p.m.	p.m.
							2 20
Grimsby .... dep.	..	5 30	9 40	..	..	1 15	2 45
London (via Boston) ...... „	..	..	9 0	..	..		
Pet....oro' (via Boston) ...... „	..	..	10 50	..	..	4 30	
Spalding (via Boston) ...... „	..	..	11 32	..	..	5 15	
Boston .... „	..	9 30	1 15	..	..	6 0	
York .... „	..	..	..	12 30	..	..	
Leeds .... „	..	7 5	..	1 0	..	..	
Doncaster .... „	..	8 0	..	2 2	..	..	
Nottingham .... „	..	8 35	..	2 5	..	..	
Grantham .... „	..	9 23	..	3 30	..	..	
					B		
Lincoln (via Honington) .. „	..	8 10	..	1 45	3 0	..	
Lincoln (via Boston) ...... „			11 5		..	3 30	
	1 2 3	1 2 3	1 2 3	1 2 3		1 2 3	
Sleaford .... „	6 0	10 30	1 52	4 15	..	6 50	
Scredington .... „	6 10	10 40	2 0	4 25	..	7 0	
Billingboro' .... „	6 30	11 12	2 12	4 40	..	7 15	
Rippingale .... „	6 45	11 20	2 20	4 55	..	7 25	
Morton .... „	6 55	11 27	2 27	5 5	..	7 35	
Bourne .... arr.	7 5	11 37	2 37	5 15	..	7 45	
Spalding .... „	10 10	..	3 5	7 0	..	..	
Lynn .... „	1 30	..	4 52	..	..	..	
Peterboro' (via Spalding) .... „				8 10	..	..	
London (via Spalding) .... „				10 10	..	..	
Essendine .... „	8 30	12 0	4 37	6 45	..	..	
Stamford .... „	8 57	12 25	5 3	7 20	..	..	
Peterboro' (via Essendine).... „	9 0	12 38	5 58	7 25	..	..	
London (via Essendine) .... „	11 43	3 35	8 10	9 20	..	..	

B Friday

This Table is issued subject to the Notices and Conditions in the Company's larger Time Bills exhibited at their se...rs

KING'S CROSS STATION,
December, 1871.

WATERLOW & SONS, PRINTERS, 'A'

Opening Timetable for the branch

NING
THE
AFORD BRANCH
ERVICE,
UARY 1872,
R NOTICE:—

DOWN.—WEEK DAYS.

		a.m.	a.m.	noon.	p.m.	p.m.
London (via Essendine)	dep.	..	7 40	12 0	..	5 0
Peterboro' (via Essendine)	„	..	9 50	1 56	..	6 43
Stamford	„	..	9 45	2 0	..	6 45
Essendine	„	..	10 20	2 20	..	7 10
Lynn	„	..	..	..	..	3 5
Spalding	„	..	8 50	..	..	5 45
		1 2 3	1 2 3	1 2 3	1 2 3	1 2 3
Bourne	„	7 30	10 45	2 55	5 40	8 0
Morton	„	7 38	10 52	3 5	5 50	8 10
Rippingale	„	7 48	11 0	3 15	6 0	8 20
						arr.
Billingboro'	„	8 5	11 13	3 30	6 15	8 40
Scredington	„	8 15	11 25	3 40	6 25	..
Sleaford	arr.	8 30	11 38	3 50	6 35	..
Lincoln (via Honington)	„	9 42	..	..	8 55	
Lincoln (via Boston)	„	..	1 40	..	..	
Grantham	„	9 10	2 35	..	7 15	
Nottingham	„	10 12	3 28	..	8 5	
Doncaster	„	11 55	4 15	..	9 8	
Leeds	„	1 11	5 15	..	10 5	
York	„	1 10	5 20	..	10 10	
Peterboro' (via Grantham)	„	10 0	3 31	..	8 20	
London (via Grantham)	„	11 50	5 30	..	10 10	
Boston	„	11 10	12 13	4 38	..	
Spalding (via Boston)	„	..	1 3	5 24	..	
Peterboro' (via Boston)	„	..	1 40	6 10	..	
London (via Boston)	„	..	4 0	8 10	..	
Grimsby	„	..	2 20	8 0	..	

s only.

l Stations.   The Classes of Trains shewn in this Table refer only to the Bourne and Sleaford Branch Trains.

HENRY OAKLEY, General Manager.

RPENTERS' HALL, LONDON WALL.

Description of the line

Sleaford

Sleaford is an important market town and road junction in south central Lincolnshire. Sited by a ford over the River Slea, it lay on a Roman road – Mareham Lane – running from Bourne towards Lincoln, and was itself a Roman community. The town is now served by the modern A15 and A17 main roads and a number of secondary routes as well as the railways between Grantham and Boston and between Spalding and Lincoln. A castle was constructed in 1130. It was later demolished, but the market, established at about the same time, was a very important one in the mid-19th Century, when the local population numbered several thousand.

Railways arrived there on 13 June 1857, when the Boston, Sleaford and Midland Counties Railway (BS&MC) opened their line from Grantham to a temporary terminus in the town.

The BS&MC was the successor to the Ambergate, Nottingham, Boston and Eastern Junction, which had been planned to run from Nottingham to Boston by way of Grantham and Folkingham, with a branch to Sleaford. The Ambergate ran out of money after it completed the section from Nottingham to Grantham, but the BS&MC took over the project and completed it, but with Sleaford on the main line rather than on a branch. The arrival of a railway in the town was greeted with the usual local enthusiasm.

'From an early hour on the morning of Saturday the population were astir. The church bells commenced ringing at half past seven o'clock and continued their joyous peals throughout the day. At intervals a band of music perambulated through the town. All the shops and places of business were closed, and the inhabitants, men, women and children were invited to partake of the festivities that were liberally provided for them. At the goods station a splendid banquet was prepared for the directors, their ladies, and friends. In the cricket ground adjoining were erected marquees inclosing long lines of tables upon which were profusely laid all the accessories needed to constitute a good and substantial dinner for the working classes of the town and its neighbourhood.'

The continuation of the line through to Boston, by way of Heckington and Swineshead, opened just under two years later, on 12 April 1859. The extension got off to an unfortunate start, when a train from Grantham ran into coal wagons being moved across the running lines without authority by the staff of a local coal merchant.

Sleaford station in G N days. Author collection

The whole line through to Boston was initially laid as single track, but the increasing traffic made doubling essential. The process began in 1873, but did not affect Sleaford until 1 June 1877 when it was doubled to Heckington, followed by a section towards Ancaster on July 1880 and the whole line by May 9 1881.

In addition to the usual benefits that the arrival of a railway brought to a town, the new facility helped Sleaford continue to be an important agricultural centre, although the locals were not always impressed by the increased numbers of cattle being walked up the main street from the station to the local cattle market. The presence of the railways helped to promote the development of major seed businesses in the town, particularly Charles Sharpe and Co, a major seed supplier to growers at home and abroad until late in the 20th Century. Sharpe's Express, a potato variety developed by the company is still popular with amateur growers more than a century after its introduction. Hubbard and Phillips was another major seed producer, and the town also became the base for a large Bass malting operation, described later.

Services to and through Sleaford were operated from the beginning by the Great Northern Railway, which took over the BS&MC on 1 January 1865. The GN had just obtained permission for a link from its Lincoln to Grantham line, and was about to gain approval for the line from

Sleaford to Bourne. As was mentioned earlier, the connection to the Grantham line was never built, and the company tried to abandon the Bourne route, but Parliament refused to permit the change, and the line opened in 1872.

The GN change of heart followed an agreement with the Great Eastern Railway to build the Great Northern and Great Eastern Joint Railway, from Spalding to Lincoln, which obviated the GN's scheme for its own additional North-South line. The Joint passed to the east of Sleaford, but was connected into the town in 1882 by a link from the south to the route from Boston, and a new section from the station running round the town to the west before re-joining the Joint just north of it. The station facilities were extended at that time.

The Bourne branch was served by Platform 3 at Sleaford station and was controlled by Sleaford East signal box. Trains leaving passed over the level crossing just to the east of the station, then ran alongside and to the south of Sleaford Junction, the point at which trains going south on the Great Northern

C12 No 4528 on Bourne train at Sleaford station in 1927. J Kite

RCH plan of Sleaford Junctions

and Great Eastern Joint Railway diverged from the original line continuing towards Boston. It provided the connection into the Bass Maltings, then continued to follow the GN&GE link before turning south just before the ballast pits near Sleaford South signal box on the Joint.

A further branch was added in 1916 to serve the RNAS airship station HMS Daedalus at Cranwell. The premises later became the RAF College, the world's first air academy.

The Bass Maltings

A series of sidings opening from a west facing junction with the branch served eight malt houses built for the Bass Brewery of Burton upon Trent. Constructed in the early years of the 20th century, they were, and may still be, the largest group of malt houses in England.

The Bass Maltings at Sleaford in recent years. At that time track could still be seen inset into the roadways around the buildings Author photograph

The business took barley from Lincolnshire and beyond, thanks to its good railway connections, and turned it into malt, the basic ingredient of beer. The location also proved to have good supplies of the right quality of water needed for the process. The grain is first dried, and then steeped in water to encourage it to start to sprout. After sprouting, the grain is allowed to grow on for a few days while being dried before being completely dried and 'toasted' to achieve the necessary consistency of malt. In a final process, the malt is then smoked over a perforated floor.

Traffic to the plant included the grain itself and the coal needed to power the machinery and provide the heat needed during the malting process. The coal used was best quality Welsh anthracite, which gave a cleaner burn more suited to a food processing operation. Wagons left the complex carrying the finished malt. A by-product of the process is malt residue, consisting of unsprouted grains and other material left over from the process. This is used as animal feed, and may have been taken away by rail, or sold to local farmers. Given the size of the Sleaford plant, the residue would probably have gone for further processing into commercial products

The Sleaford maltings remained in business until more modern technology rendered it redundant, and it closed in 1959. Grade 1 listed, it has struggled to find new uses, and has been damaged by fire several times. At the time of writing, its future is still in doubt.

Burton Siding

Burton Siding existed to serve the Burton Brick and Tile Works of the Fen Brick Company, also known as the Willoughby Brick Works, which had brick pits and working facilities between Mareham Lane and the railway. The siding left the line just north of a level crossing on the road from Burton Pedwardine to Silk Willoughby.

J2 locomotive 65020 and train passing the Burton Brick Works in about 1950. Photo F W Page

Aswarby and Scredington

Aswarby and Scredington station. Author collection

Originally named Scredington for Aswarby, this station, as with three of the four on the line wasn't really convenient for the villages it served. The half mile to the centre of Scredington was probably fairly standard for the days when most people walked everywhere, but the three miles to Aswarby is a little more surprising given that that village is not much further from the larger rail-head of Sleaford.

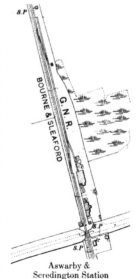

Scredington had just under 400 inhabitants, mostly involved in farming, although the trades represented in 1882 include brickmaking, two public houses, one of them the Brickmaker's Arms, a blacksmith, a shoemaker and two shopkeepers. Aswarby had only 150, many of them in the direct or indirect employ of Sir Thomas Whichcote, of Aswarby Hall. They included a stone mason, a gamekeeper, a stud groom and a gardener, all considered important enough to be named in that's year's White's Directory, as was the local blacksmith who was also the postmaster. Sir Thomas's brother, Rev Christopher was the local vicar, and the prominence of the Whichcotes may well be a reason for the railway connection.

The station was served by a loop of track with a single siding running by a loading dock and into a brick-built goods shed. A

Aswarby &
Scredington Station

19

signal box at the south end of the station also controlled the Station Road level crossing.

Heavy snows in the area in the early part on 1922 stopped traffic along the line, with six-foot drifts at Scredington the main obstacle.

The ending of the passenger service in 1930 saw older children from the village, who attended school in Billingborough, lose a small perk of their location. The return train service had left Billingborough at 3.40pm, which meant they had to be allowed to leave the school before the 4pm end of classes. The replacement 'Welcome' bus waited until the end of the session, permitting them to 'enjoy' the full day at school.

Billingborough and Horbling

Billingborough and Horbling station lay unusually close for this line, just to the west of the large village of Billingborough and a mile south of Horbling. It also claimed to be the railhead for the small but ancient market town of Folkingham, some 4 miles away, Billingborough was the largest community served by the line, with 1227 persons listed on the 1871 census, and Horbling added a further 578. The two villages shared a gas works and a Mutual Improvement Society, although both were based in Billingborough. The chair of the Society was a Dr Blasson, also surgeon to the railway company. Billingborough had a church and four chapels as well as a 'large and commodious' public hall.

Billingborough and Horbling station in about 1900. Author collection

Billingborough supported a full range of local services, including a 'milliner and fancy repository'; an 'ironmonger, iron & tin plate worker, brazier and gas fitter, and agent for agricultural implements'; a ladies boarding school and a watch and clock maker who was also the local taxidermist. Several pubs and beer houses were in operation, with the Fortescue Hotel offering 'a fly or day cart' on hire for onward travellers, and Thomas Casswell paid tribute to the railway by running the Great Northern Brewery. Horbling had three inns, one of which was also the post office, eleven farmers, three boot and shoe makers, a blacksmith and two solicitors.

The station was under the control of Clerk in Charge William Jackson and offered a passing loop in the station as well as a goods loop serving a goods shed and loading bay. Two signal boxes were situated at the north and south ends of the station. Each controlled a level crossing over the Folkingham and Birthorpe roads respectively. There were also two long sidings where coal merchants Joseph Gibson and William Dods both had loading and storage facilities. Robert Taylor also operated in the station yard as a coal, linseed cake, salt & lime merchant, while John Sinclair had a coal, animal feed and manure business. Mt Sinclair suffered a theft from his premises, according to the Grantham Journal of 9 November 1872 when a 'carpenter of Billingborough was charged with stealing coal from the railway station at Billingborough, on the 7th'.

The same paper did report better news for the railway in that it was proving popular for excursions and special trips.

6th July 1872. District items. Billingborough 'The Spalding Show, During the three days exhibition of the Agricultural Show, 495 passengers booked from Billingborough station for Spalding.'

'May Fair. On Monday last over 590 persons were booked from this station; four hundred and seventy five were booked by one train, being the largest number ever despatched by one train since the line has been opened.' Grantham Journal 23rd May 1874.

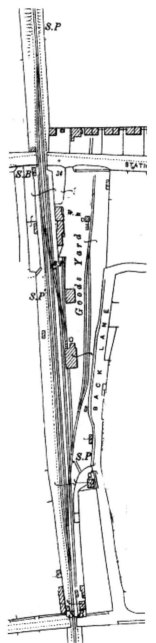

The station suffered at least one accident in its early days

Horse shunting at Billingborough. Fraser Ross

'During shunting operations on Wednesday afternoon some wagons attached to a Great Northern goods train fouled the points. Two laden with granite from the Groby Company were completely overturned and another derailed. The smash blocked one line of rails and passenger traffic had to be worked over the down line. A breakdown gang was engaged all the afternoon in clearing away the obstruction. One of the overturned wagons was badly smashed and damage was done to the permanent way.'

Level crossing gates regularly suffered damage, although the incident in December 1891 was a more serious event.

Billingborough North signal box alongside the Folkingham Road crossing. Richard Goodman

'Accident on the railway – On Monday evening the six o'clock goods train ran into and smashed one of the massive gates at the Falkingham Road level crossing adjoining Billingboro' station. From what we can gather, the accident was entirely due to the carelessness on the part of the driver. The gates were quite new having been hung on the introduction of the block system a few months ago.' Stamford Mercury.

The size of the station, and its central location made it a convenient base for permanent way workers. Graham Morfoot remembered then from post-WW2 days.

Wickham trolley shed. Graham Morfoot

"There was a PW gang at Billingborough with a Wickham trolley stored in a line side shed close to Birthorpe Road crossing. I remember regularly visiting the wooden shed in the station yard where there always seemed to be a fire in the cast iron stove, and the smell of creosote in the air as they burned old sleepers. They won the award for best kept section in the region one year, can't remember the year, very proud men at the time."

Millthorpe siding

Millthorpe might seem to be an unusual location for a siding. The community itself only had 72 inhabitants in 1872, and was regarded as part of the larger village of Aslackby. Two farmers are the only inhabitants to make it on to White's list of local notables in that year. The siding ran north from Millthorpe Drove on the west of the line, close to the hamlet. It had facilities for unloading loose materials such as coal, stone and fertiliser, and would have been used for

outgoing farm produce such as potatoes and vegetables also sugar beet after WW1.

A small signal cabin controlled the siding and the crossing. It boasted an unusual 'Hayrake' lever frame made by Ransom & Rapier in the 1870s, mostly found in south Lincolnshire.

Millthorpe Siding cabin. Mr Packford in charge. R Tarpey collection

The much larger village of Pointon lay less than half a mile north of the siding, which may well have served as a goods railhead for it, Aslackby and Dowsby. Pete Bristow, whose family farmed down Pointon Fen, used Millthorpe for loading sugar beet.

The siding saw one of the earliest accidents on the line involving passengers when a carriage wheel became derailed in November 1872 while passing over the points there. The train stopped, the wheel was 'placed in its proper position' by the train staff, allowing it to continue on its way.

The Hay-rake frame at Millthorpe.
Brian Lawrence collection

A very similar incident took place on an embankment near Horbling the following year when an axle broke on a coal wagon. The train was 'well-filled with passengers returning from Grantham Stock Sale and Sleaford Market' and the report on the incident suggested that if the coupling on the wagon had not held the passenger carriages might have rolled over and down the embankment. Fortunately, it did hold, and the train was stopped by the joint efforts of the engine driver and the guards, for whom the passengers took a collection on the spot.

Passengers were once again inconvenienced at Millthorpe in January 1901.

'Traffic on the Bourne and Sleaford line of the Great Northern Railway was considerably disorganised …. owing to the breakdown of a goods train at Millthorpe siding. One of the principal valves of the engine burst and the train was unable to proceed. The line was blocked for several hours. Two of the afternoon trains were cancelled and it was not until evening that there was a proper restoration of traffic. The mishap occasioned much delay and inconvenience to passengers.'

No collection was recorded on this occasion.

Rippingale.

A large and pleasant village, according to White's 'on a gentle acclivity, near the Folkingham road, being 3 miles S. of Folkingham, and 5 miles N. of Bourn'. There were 690 residents in 1872. St. Andrew's church and two Methodist chapels looked after the religious needs of the

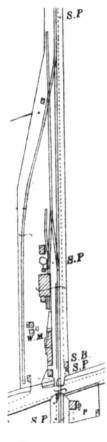

Rippingale station in 1905 with the train to Bourne approaching. The poster advertises a trip to the Test Match at Trent Bridge, Nottingham. Author collection

locals. John Caunco and Miss Jane Hind educated the children, although Mr Caunco found time to run a shop as well. Most of the remaining local needs were catered for by a windmill, several inns, two blacksmiths, two wheelwrights, three bakers, two cobblers. a saddler, two butchers, a tailor and two drapers, two carpenters, one gardener and William Wilson, who is simply described as a drill owner, presumably a piece of agricultural machinery.

William North was the local coal dealer and most likely worked from the long siding in the station yard, which opened from the north end of a loop that also provided access to a goods shed and loading platform.

As with other stations on the line, excursions were a regular feature at Rippingale, although the trip to Skegness by 'the juvenile members of the Gladstone Benefit Society' proved less than satisfactory. Despite leaving the village in 'glorious sunshine' it was raining at the coast and 'no better weather awaited them at their return, when several had to walk from the station'.

Rippingale church choir waiting to depart on an outing in 1905. Brian Lawrence collection

Track gang with trolley at Rippingale station. Brian Lawrence collection

Hacconby siding

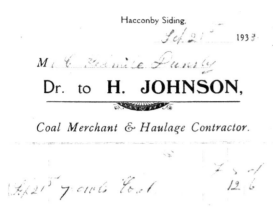

Hacconby Siding.

Sep 21 1933

M. C. Beatrice Family

Dr. to **H. JOHNSON,**

Coal Merchant & Haulage Contractor.

Sep 21 7 cwt Coal   12 6

Hacconby siding lay on the eastern edge of Hacconby village, a fairly substantial community of nearly 500 people in 1872. It had petitioned for a station when the line was being built, but it was turned down by GN due to its proximity to Morton and Rippingale. The siding ran north from Hacconby Drove and lay on the west side of the through tracks. It was controlled by a signal box by the level crossing

The facilities and traffic would have been similar to those at Millthorpe, although a coal merchant, H Johnson, operated a business from there.

Morton Road

Station Rd, Morton. The station is in the far distance.
Author collection

The name gives the location away again. Morton Road station was about half a mile from the village centre on the road out to Morton Fen, although the community has now expanded to cover the old station site. In 1872 the village population was 973, including the hamlet of Hanthorpe which lies on the other side of the main Bourne to Sleaford road. As is usually the case in these fen-edge villages, farming was the main occupation, with 21 farmers listed by name in Whites of that year.

Three publicans are shown, as are William Kenney and William Thurlby, who traded as grocers and maltsters, and may have provided some of the raw material to the brewers. Three blacksmiths, two wheelwrights, a saddler, a brickmaker and a wool and seed merchant served the farming community. All the usual commercial trades and businesses are represented, including a glass and china dealer, although Jesse Stow seems to have been particularly busy as the National schoolmaster, land surveyor, rate collector, vestry clerk, organist and agent to the Briton Insurance Company. Robert Ward was listed as a market gardener, and George Ward, possibly a relation, was the county police officer.

The station layout was similar to that at Rippingale. Wagons carrying milk churns needed to be sure of swift passage, and were attached to passenger trains by being rolled down the yard under the influence of gravity

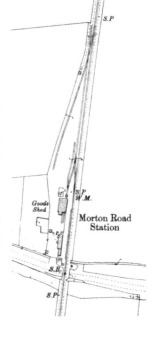

Bourn Junction, later Bourne East Junction

Following a modification of the plans in 1871, a connection was made of the single line branch to both tracks of the Midland and Eastern at a point '3 chains east of the turnpike from Bourn to Market Deeping' – now the A15 road – and about 150 yards from the station. The junction was controlled by Bourne East signal box.

Bourne

Another well-established south Lincolnshire market town notable as the home of Hereward the Wake, an Anglo-Saxon leader who opposed the Conquest of England by William I. According to legend, Hereward took to the fens to the south and east of the town to fight the Norman invaders.

Bourne became a significant railway junction in the second half of the 19th century by virtue of an accumulation of services delivered by a number of small companies. The first, albeit at a distance of two miles from the town, was the Edenham and Little Bytham Railway, built by Lord Willoughby de Eresby across his estates at Grimsthorpe. It ran from a junction with the Great Northern Railway at Little Bytham to the village of Edenham, also serving the village and castle at Grimsthorpe.

The line opened in 1856 for goods, with a passenger service starting in December of the following year. Passenger carriages were built for the E&LB by the Great Northern, but the latter declined to operate the line, a sensible view in the light of two failures of inspection by the Board of Trade, low passenger usage and a tendency of Lord Willoughby's son, Albyric, to commandeer the train whenever he needed to get to the main line, or be collected from it. Coal and other commodities for Bourne were carried on the line, and then moved from Edenham to Bourne by road. Three locomotives, Ophir, a converted traction engine, Havilah and Columbia worked the line.

Passenger services ended in October 1871, with goods continuing for a few more years, eventually using horse haulage for the trains, rather than locomotives.

The principal reason for closure was the loss of traffic to the first railway to serve the town of Bourne itself, the Essendine and Bourne Railway, opened on 16 June 1860 between Bourne and another station on the GN main line, Essendine, which was also the junction for a branch to Stamford, opened four years earlier. Connections could be made at Stamford for onward movement by the Midland Railway, on its line from Peterborough to Melton Mowbray. Both companies maintained their own stations in Stamford, so although goods could move between both on a link line, passengers had to disembark from the one to reach the other. The Bourne and Essendine served two intermediate stations at Thurlby and Braceborough Spa.

J6 No 4220 passing under Carlby Bridge on the Essendine to Bourne line. Rev. David Creasey

The Spalding and Bourne Railway opened its line from the east into the town in 1866. Despite passing through sparsely inhabited farmland, it provided three intermediate stations, at Twenty, Counter Drain and North Drove. After a number of agreements and mergers this became part of the Midland and Eastern Railway, later the Midland and Great Northern Joint Railway, operated by a committee from the two parent companies. East of Spalding, the M&GN served a number of south Lincolnshire communities before crossing into Norfolk where its network covered much of the north of that county.

The next connection into Bourne was the line dealt with in this book – the GN's branch from Sleaford, which arrived in January 1872. As mentioned earlier, the original plans for that line had envisaged a connection with the GN's line to Essendine to the west of Bourne, but joining the Midland and Eastern allowed a simpler connection with less expensive building costs.

On leaving Bourne, the line crossed a long, low bridge over the River Glen and an adjacent drain. In October 1880 the banks of the Glen burst, flooding the line and land to the west of it. The line was then closed to all traffic, not opening again until 1 February the following year.

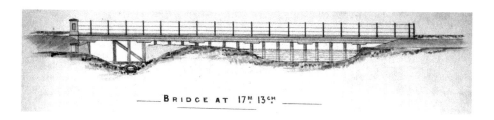

BRIDGE AT 17ᴹ 13ᶜʰ

Drawing of the River Glen Bridge at Bourne

Shortly after the Sleaford connection went in, another set of crossing gates, those at Bourne, took a battering.

'The return excursion train …… arrived at Bourne between three and four o'clock on Sunday morning [30 March]. When near the platform at Bourne station the engine came into violent collision with two empty carriages which were standing upon the line, driving them completely through two very strong gates at the South Street crossing, one of the gates being smashed to splinters, and the carriages considerably damaged. There were nine passengers (including two ladies) in the carriage attached to the engine but we have not heard of anyone sustaining greater injury than a severe shaking. One gentleman's hat was smashed to such an extent that he has put in a claim for a new one.' Grantham Journal.

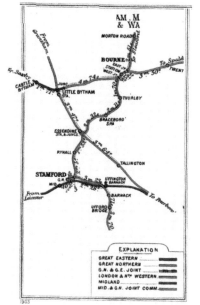

The final link came in on Mayday 1894 when a new connection with the Midland Railway at Saxby was completed by the M&GN, avoiding the need for a detour through Essendine and Stamford for goods and passengers headings for Melton Mowbray and beyond. The M&GN then became famous for its express services from the towns and cities around Nottingham, Derby and Leicester to the seaside resorts on the North Norfolk coast.

An unusual feature of Bourne station was the use of the Red Hall, a Tudor mansion built in the early 1600s, as the booking offices and Station Master's residence. It was connected to the island platform by a footbridge over the lines.

Bourne 1950s M&GN train at platform, 5MT and J6 locos in the yard. Rev. David Creasey

A large goods shed and locomotive facilities were provided and the station handled substantial amounts of farm produce including livestock and arable crops from the good grazing land of the Heath to the west and the more fertile silt and peat Fens to the east.

The Red Hall at Bourne, used as station offices. The station itself can be seen to the left of the building. The footbridge for passengers is also visible. Author collection

32

The Line in Operation

The initial service on the line in January 1872 consisted of four trains a day each way between Bourne and Sleaford, stopping at all stations along the way, with the final service out of Bourne only going as far as Billingborough. Three classes of service were available on all trains, with third class reportedly carried on what were effectively goods wagons. An extra train in each direction was added the following month, with the late Bourne-Billingborough service extended to Sleaford as from November in that year.

Tickets & luggage labels from the branch

Grantham Journal 'Alterations in the train service - There are several important alterations in the train system for November on the Great Northern Railway including, -

Bourne and Sleaford branch The 7.45 pm train, Bourne to Billingborough will be continued to Sleaford, arriving Scredington 8.25 pm and Sleaford 8-30pm.'

Two trains a day each way also served stations between Bourne and Essendine, on the GN main line.

The first trains of the day were particularly relevant on market days, as shown by the GN's action when a market was cancelled.

Christmas 1872 'The Great Northern Railway Company have given notice that as there will be no market at Sleaford on Boxing Day, they will not run the early train from Bourn. For the same reason, cheap market tickets will not be issued on Monday.'

In 1873, the service reduced back to five a day, but all of them served the whole line.

1873 also saw a price war break out between the established fuel merchants along the line, and a new Coal and Coke Cooperative Society set up to serve local customers. The locals seem to have won out, since references to the Cooperative do not appear in local records.

Increased travel to and from the area became apparent very quickly. 6-700 passengers arrived by rail to the well-established Stow Green Horse Fair in 1873, and seaside excursions, initially to Hunstanton in Norfolk by way of the M&GN, but later to GN resorts such as Skegness became regular events.

21 September 1872 'On Wednesday (18th) last a cheap trip was run to Hunstanton, the number of persons booked being - at Scredington 19, Billingborough 57, Rippingale 25 and Morton 15.'

Some excursions were even more ambitious. A trip to Belle Vue in 1882 left Bourne at 2.50am, picking up passengers along the line to Sleaford, and didn't get back to its starting point until 3.25am the following day, although another to a six-day event in London was reportedly poorly supported.

The importance of the time tables to travellers was indicated by a note in the Spalding Free Press in 1876.

'Time Tables. As several alterations have been made this month in the times of arrivals and departures of trains from this station, our readers would do well to consult the time-tables before starting a journey, to avoid disappointment.'

The disappointment might not have been too great. The main change was in the timing of one train, which would now be leaving at 3.27 instead of 3.22.

From the late 1870s, the service settled down to what it would be for most of the time that a passenger service was offered – 5 or 6 passenger trains each way, each day, with an early train from Bourne on Mondays to serve Sleaford market. A single dedicated goods train ran every day each way, stopping at all stations but several of the passenger services were mixed trains that also carried goods. The Working Time Table for 1882 showed 7 trains a day, of which 3 were just passenger, 2 were passenger, goods and coal, one was passengers and goods and the other just goods and coal. Passenger trains could have up to six cattle wagons attached and mixed trains were allowed up to be up to ten vehicles in length, not including the passenger carriages.

Services reduced slightly during WW1, with 4 passenger trains a day in 1915, but back up to 5 by 1917.

Sleaford train leaving Bourne behind a GNR E2 class locomotive. R Tarpey collection

The railway took part in the 1918 celebration of the Armistice that ended the First World War, when a 'feu-de-joie' - a rifle salute with guns firing in succession to give a near-continuous sound - was fired at Billingborough station.

The same welcome awaited the Billingborough football team two years later when it arrived back at the station there after beating Bourne 2-0 in the Ancaster Cup. 200+ supporters had travelled to Bourne by train for the match, with another 100 joining it at Rippingale. Bert Foston, in his book 'Billingborough Memories, reported that the train stopped half a mile out of Billingborough station to allow the team captain and one other member to ride in on the front buffer beam, carrying the Cup. Health and Safety was a more relaxed requirement in those days.

Bert took a different view to the value of the post-WW1 railway to my grandfather. Rather than the slow and useless service Grandpa considered it to be, Bert described it as 'second to none' and the village's 'greatest asset'.

'Everyone used it, for passengers and for goods in and out of the village. Rail travel was great and the only way of keeping in touch with the outside world'.

'There were special trips to the ever popular Nottingham Goose Fair, Lincoln Christmas shopping, evening jaunts, one shilling return to the seaside and back, Skegness 2/6 (12.5p) return for the whole day. The whole village would go.'

A coal strike in 1912 saw a reduction in services, but that in 1921 caused major difficulties to the railway company and the locals. The train service was reduced in April, and cut back to two a day in May. At the same time, the local gas works in Billingborough ran short of coal and first rationed the gas supply then closed the works in June. Following the end of the strike, things returned to normal in July. At that time, 4 passenger trains and one goods ran each way along the line, with two passengers serving Essendine as well, and the goods working out of Grantham by way of Sleaford. Harold Bonnet, in his book 'Smoke and Steam', described being tested as a fireman in November 1925 on the Grantham-Bourne run by way of Sleaford. The locomotive concerned was LNER 4155, an 0-6-0 tender loco rebuilt in 1924 from a GNR J4 as an LNER J3.

J3 64137 at Burton Siding c1950. F W Page

One unfortunate traveller in the summer of 1930 found himself both injured and fined after an incident at Billingborough. An Irishman, on his way to a village just off the line was told that he would be nearer his destination of he continued to the next station, Rippingale. He therefore returned to his seat and dozed off. The train moved on, but only as far as the cattle dock, and the traveller, woken by the train stopping, thought he was at Rippingale, so opened the door and jumped out. There being no platform alongside him, he fell to the ground, suffering bruises and a sprained wrist. Since opening a door when not in a station was an offence, he was later fined 5/- (25p) with 10/- (50p) costs, although a sympathetic fellow passenger did pay his costs.

Passenger numbers were never high on the branch, and any connections it offered through Sleaford or Bourne were generally better served by other lines from those towns. The LNER therefore proposed the closure of passenger service on it, and on a number of other poorly supported routes. They argued that the Lincolnshire Road Car bus company, which was partially owned by the railway company, would be able to provide the necessary service. Milk, eggs and butter for the local markets, which were normally carried by passenger train, would be moved by lorry, and parcel delivery in the villages was delayed by an hour to allow them to be carried on the milk lorries and delivered with the general mail. Passenger traffic ended in 1930, with the last train running on the 20th September, although special Sunday excursions to Skegness and other coastal location continued occasionally until the outbreak of WW2. John Richardson, a farmer from Morton Fen, remembered that they were popular with farm workers. The day trips, he said were often 'the only holiday that a lot of then had'.

CLOSING OF BRANCH LINES—BOURNE & SLEAFORD BRANCH—L.N.E.R.

On and from the 22nd September, 1930, the Passenger train service on the above-mentioned branch will be withdrawn, and through booking of passengers to Morton Road, Rippingale, Billingboro' and Aswarby stations will be discontinued from that date.

The conveyance of merchandise and live-stock by Goods train, and of parcels, milk, fruit and other miscellaneous traffic including live-stock charged at rates applicable to passenger train or other similar service will be continued. Particulars of the service for such traffic will be obtainable at stations on the Branch Line.

Attention is drawn to the omnibus services operated between Bourne and Sleaford by the Lincolnshire Road Car Company Ltd., full particulars of which are obtainable from the local station masters.

F.R. 6/Pad. 22.

Manning level crossings on rural lines were a constant drain on railway company finances. Above is in the hamlet of Dyke, close to Bourne and right is thought to be south of Scredington. Author collection

Goods Only

After the end of passenger service, which had regularly carried goods vehicles as well as passenger coaches, the goods service needed to be increased to two trains a day each way, with an extra available on Mondays if needed for Sleaford market business.

Goods at that time would have included coal, coke, fertiliser and stone in bulk incoming, as well as whole train-loads of seed potatoes from Scotland before the spring planting season. Outgoing would have been potatoes, sugar beet, bagged grain, often in sacks hired from the railway company, and other agricultural crops.

GNR goods vehicles in Billingborough station. St Andrew's church in background. Fraser Ross

John Richardson remembered Morton station as being a busy place at certain times of the year, with two porters, employed to deal with goods even after the end of passenger service.

Hay being delivered to Billingborough station by steam-hauled wagons. Fraser Ross

"Jim Taylor, my farm foreman, told me that in about 1936, in the autumn, when they were loading sacks of wheat and taking back seed potatoes, with other people putting on sugar beet and potatoes, he counted 70 horses on carts and wagons in Morton station yard, and it continued that way right to the end of the war. With petrol being rationed almost everything coming into the farm and going away went by train."

Horses were needed by most of the farmers along the line well into post-WW2 years, and although the majority were bred on the farms, some replacements were brought in from elsewhere. A special trade that James Measures, of Dowsby was involved in every year was the arrival of Clydesdale horses bought at the Carlisle sales by his father, who preferred the slightly lighter Clydesdales to the more usual shires. The horses were then despatched from Carlisle to Lincolnshire by train.

"In those days my father had over 100 working horses on the farms and he would buy twelve or sixteen to replace some of the older ones. I remember as a teenager – it would have been the 1940s – waiting at Rippingale station for them, often late at night. We would each take four horses, one on each side with a halter and another one fastened to each of those, and walk them to the farm – we never had a problem because there was no traffic. You just had to learn to walk putting one foot in front of the other because if one stepped on your foot, he wouldn't move that foot until he had moved all the others, and you knew what colour your toes would be the next day!"

The author's grandfather, Herbert Stennett, with a decorated wagon in Billingborough station yard. Author collection

Seed potatoes came from Scotland packed in sacks and carried in box vans in batches of ten tonnes, but John Richardson reported that getting them off the wagons could be difficult.

"With all the shaking on the way, and the shunting and the movement, the bags would settle down and pack together and be very hard to pull out. The Scotsmen would also pack about a foot of barley straw onto the top of the load to keep the frost off the potatoes, but the barley awns would all work into your clothes and under your arms and be very uncomfortable."

General operations during the war changed very little from peacetime traffic, although the local potato crop, and its associated rail carriage, increased substantially as grassland was ploughed up and used for the crop. One goods a day each way ran in 1942, but extras were added for potato carriage. An operating regulation at the time was that vegetable traffic going to London by way of Spalding and Peterborough had to be marshalled next to the

40

engine. Blackout restrictions on lights and fires at night caught out a worker at Rippingale station, who was accused of allowing a rubbish fire to set light to grass in the vicinity. He was fined 10/- for his misdemeanour despite colleagues testifying that he had extinguished the flames.

Billingborough station was used by the United States Air Force to bring in equipment for Folkingham aerodrome, which was only a couple of miles away. Unloading large items of equipment onto big road vehicles into a small station yard with awkward road access caused many problems there and in the village.

Loading potatoes from sacks on a wagon into railway trucks.
Author collection

After the war, the line continued to serve the goods needs of the area. Peter Wakefield, who lived at Billingborough station while his father was station master there in the 1950s described how goods trains could leave there for Sleaford with 60 loaded wagons, the maximum allowed behind 'a valiant J6'. He remembered the 'great excitement' of a farmer moving his equipment lock stock and barrel to Norfolk – my father also moved some of his farm equipment from Billingborough to North Nottinghamshire in 1956. An unusual trade was when a local mattress company would send a van-load of feathers to London – a 12-ton van would carry a ton of feathers!

Sugar beet remained important. Andrew Pilgrim and his father grew the crop in the early sixties.

"We would knock and top the beet in the field and load the trailer behind our little grey Fergie and then off to Billingborough station. I have seen dad move the wagons on the line by hand using a long piece of wood with a metal end on it. Dad also told me of the time he carted sugar beet to the station using a donkey and tub trap after his shire horse died between the shafts of his cart while pulling beet to the station."

Graham Morfoot also remembered taking wagon loads of sugar beet behind a Ferguson tractor to be loaded by hand into wagons at the loading platform/bay.

"Most farmers used rail to send beet to Spalding. During the campaign there was always at least one wagon being loaded or ready for pick up."

"Bagged spuds, beans, peas and wheat were all going out and coal coming in to the merchants. The coke for my father's bakery ovens came by rail."

A less pleasant memory was that of loads of guano, dried sea-bird droppings used as agricultural fertiliser. It came as grey granules with a terrible smell.

An unusual traffic remembered by Mrs Ruth Measures, from Dowsby, was fox hounds.

"When the Belvoir Hunt was meeting round here, they would bring the hounds from the hunt kennels to Billingborough, or sometimes Rippingale, to ensure that they were fresh for the chase."

The Belvoir Hunt at Billingborough Station

John Richardson remembered the railway service as being comprehensive if occasionally erratic.

"We went off by train in a January for a skiing holiday, but my case got lost on the way back. I heard nothing for some time, until the end of February, when the British Rail lorry came round delivering sugar beet seed, and I spotted my case on the lorry. It was very battered, and where it had been I don't know, but I was very glad to get it back!"

Passenger excursions ran occasionally from stations on the line. Your author remembers his regret when he was taken to Liverpool in 1951 to see the new cathedral there while some of his class-mates got to go to visit the Festival of Britain in London! Peter Wakefield travelled on that one from Billingborough to Kings Cross by way of Bourne and Essendine He was 10 at the time, and remembered the train as being 10 corridor coaches behind a J6.

The Sleaford to Billingborough section of track closed on 28 July 1956, although a continued to be used as storage for redundant wagons for some time. The Railway Correspondence and Travel Society (RCTS) travelled over the branch on Sunday September 9th of that year. 'The Fensman No 2' tour was a combination of two trains, one originating from London Kings Cross and the other from Nottingham. As part of that tour K2 2-6-0 61743 took the train along the branch from Sleaford to Bourne and on to Spalding.

Above. The RCTS Fensman Rail Tour entering Billingborough station 9 September 1956. Roy Harrison.   Below: The train at Willoughby Joyce. J H Platts

The situation following the partial closure can be summed up by the description of facilities in the 1956 Handbook of Stations. Aswarby and Scredington and Burton Siding were not listed, being closed.

Billingborough and Horbling was listed as the terminus of a branch from Bourne, which offered goods and

passenger facilities, even though the last passenger train left 20 years earlier, but it did not handle parcels or miscellaneous traffic, although furniture vans, livestock wagons could be accommodated as could 'carriages and motor cars', as long as they arrived attached to a (non-existent!) passenger train. Rippingale and Morton Road stations had the same facilities as Billingborough and Horbling.

Millthorpe Siding was under the control of Billingborough and Rippingale, and Hacconby Siding was similarly shared by Rippingale and Morton Road, but the only traffic either could accept was coal or minerals in truck-loads.

THURSDAY, 26th JUNE, 1958

Empty Stock

Bounds Green Sidings to King's Cross

Class .. .. —	—	—	C
			PM
Bounds Green		dep	7 55
King's Cross (No. 10 Platform) ..		arr	8 55

"GROVE" Special Train

King's Cross to Sleaford

M. C.				PM
—	King's Cross (No. 10 Platform) ..		dep	9 55
10 10	Greenwood		..	10 10
7 44	Hatfield		..	10 18
14 20	Hitchin		..	10 31½
26 76	Huntingdon North ..		..	10 53
17 39	Peterborough North ..		..	11 12
16 50	Spalding Town ..		..	11 34
18 79	Sleaford		arr	12 0
			dep	12 8
—	Sleaford (Bourne Branch) ..		arr	12 13

Restrictions

In the event of the special train having to run over the Down Slow line at New Southgate Station, the adjacent No. I Siding must be clear.
Speed not to exceed 10 m.p.h. when travelling over the Bourne Branch.

Timetable of the Royal Train London to the branch. 26 June 1959

The line had one final moment of passenger glory in June 1958, when the Royal Train, carrying Her Majesty the Queen, was stabled there overnight on the 26th. Her Majesty was on her way to Lincoln to open the new Pelham Bridge which had been built to remove a notorious traffic bottle neck at the Durham Ox level crossing at the junction of lines coming out of Lincoln's two stations. B1 4-6-0 No 60149 took the train non-stop from Kings Cross to Sleaford, while Nos 61258 & 61408 were stabled on front of train overnight, then took it on to Lincoln the following day. The train, comprising eleven carriages, left Kings Cross at 9.55pm on the 26th and arrived on the branch at just after midnight on the 27th. The driver was warned not to exceed 10mph on the branch! Departure that morning was at 09.15am to arrive in Lincoln at 10am. The branch's moment of Royal glory was over.

All traffic nearly came to an end the same year, when British Railways announced that it intended to close the M&GN through Bourne, with what was now the Billingborough branch closing as well. However, on 11 November 1958, the East Midlands Consultative Committee, meeting in Bourne, while approving the plans for Lincolnshire, instructed BR to retain Spalding to Bourne and on to Billingborough for goods.

The rest of the M&GN closed on 2 March 1959, leaving a daily weekday goods service to Billingborough which left Spalding at 9.24am, served stations from there to Bourne, arriving there at 11.13. It left for Billingborough at 11.55, arriving at 1.50pm, probably depending on the needs of the request stops at Morton Road and Rippingale. The return left at 3, arriving in Bourne at 5.15, continuing to Spalding three quarters of an hour later. Station Masters and agents were urged to make sure the return train ran to time to ensure connections at Spalding. On Saturday mornings the train left Spalding at 7.30am, but only as far as Bourne, although the Station Master there had to phone the branch stations to see if a train was required. If so, that train continued to Billingborough. From 1962, when the requirement to man all level crossings was lifted, train staff worked the gates at all locations other than stations.

D2027 at Rippingale on the Billingborough train 28 Sept 1963. John Bonser

The train crews were based at Spalding, and one looked after the service to Billingborough, before riding in the road parcels van to Sleaford to catch a train home. The return service crew also made use of the parcels van from Sleaford to take over the train at Billingborough.

The reprieve was only temporary, and goods trains between Spalding, Bourne and Billingborough ran for the last time in the spring of 1965.

Farmer James Measures, from Dowsby, remembered the last delivery of cattle onto the branch. The animals concerned had been loaded at Hexham, in Northumberland, to be brought to the Lincolnshire Fens for fattening before slaughter. They arrived in Spalding at a time the railway thought was too late to deliver to Rippingale. They offered to keep the stock overnight, giving them some food and water, but saw a potential hitch.

"I asked how much they would charge me for keeping them, and they said ten bob (50p) a head, and I said I'm not paying that, you can bring them straight away and we will wait for them to get here."

The wagons were duly moved to Bourne, and then up the branch to Rippingale, despite a heavy fog on the fen that required a member of railway staff to go in front of the train to make sure there were no obstacles on the line.

Mr Measures and two of his men were waiting 'in the little hut by the rail side – with the fire burning, of course!' at Rippingale, and despite the late hour, they then walked the cattle in the dark down the fen to their crew yards.

He felt that this must have been one of the last commercial uses of the line, since after that he only saw railway system trains checking what was there before the equipment arrived that was used to lift the tracks. Like most farmers owning land either side of the line, he bought that section of the trackbed between Dunsby and Hacconby and incorporated it into his farming business.

One record shows that the final locomotive to run on the line was a Class 08 diesel shunter hauling four vans and a brake van. Another shows the loco as No D3442, but that may just have been the shorter Saturday service from Bourne to Spalding.

John Richardson admitted that he has always regretted not persuading the train crew during the reduced service to let him ride from Morton to Billingborough and back.

"I don't know if I would have been allowed to, but it would have been worth trying."

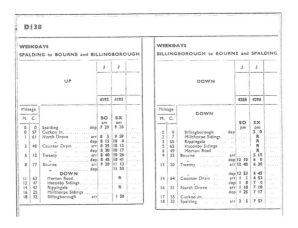

Working timetable. Winter 1961-2

Locomotives

Locomotives used in the early days were almost certainly hand-me-downs from more important GN lines, a tradition that continued through the line's existence. A report in April 1893 that a market train had failed along the line due to a piston rod breaking on locomotive No 113 noted that it 'had seen much service'. No 113 was a Hawthorn 0-4-2 goods engine built in 1849, and was taken out of service later in the year of the incident.

Locomotive No 112A, a member of the same class as No 113, which came to grief in 1893. The tender is interesting as it has survived to the present day as one of the oldest pieces of GNR equipment in preservation. Courtesy GNR Society

The line was one of a number that the GN considered for the introduction of steam railmotors, but they were only introduced to the northern part of Lincolnshire, where the inability to add coaches for occasional heavy loads proved a disadvantage. The same would most likely have been true with the Sleaford to Bourne line, where traffic was much heavier on market days.

GNR railmotor of the type considered for the branch. This example is seen at Louth. Courtesy GNR Society

G H F Benstead remembered that, during the post-WW1 years, before the GN was absorbed into the LNER in 1923, passengers services were always hauled by C2, later LNER C12, class 4-4-2 tank engines, which dated back to the late 1890s. The coaches, he added, were always 6-wheelers, with no bogie examples to be seen.

47

"The pick-up goods trains were pulled by several types of Stirling and Ivatt vintage", he went on. *"Occasionally one would see a Stirling mixed traffic 0-4-2 tender loco in action; domeless Stirling 0-6-0s and early types of Ivatt 0-6-0s, painted, pre-grouping, a darkish grey, lined white."*

Above LNER C12 No 4510 with a passenger train from Sleaford to Bourne. Fraser Ross
Below No 1529, which was based at Grantham and may have worked the branch. GNRS

The C12s remained stalwart servants on the line, with most passenger trains continuing to be hauled by them – two of Grantham's C12s, Nos 1525/7/9/33 were based at Sleaford in the late 1920s, and normally worked the branch.

GNR 0-6-0s were frequently seen on the goods and mixed trains into the 1930s and beyond, with LNER J6s and J11s and K2 2-6-0s being the kind of locos which would have caught my eye as a small boy in the years after WW2. Two of Boston's allocation of J6's were based at Sleaford in the 1950s, with one used each day for the 10.55am goods service to Bourne, returning at 3.15pm. 64212 and 64260 were spotted there in April 1956.

A J11 with a snow-plough was used to clear drifts from the line in the hard winter of 1947. Unfortunately, it also cleared the crossing keeper's hut at Millthorpe Siding in the process!

BR J6 No 64278 at Bourne in the 1950s. Rev. David Creasey

Unidentified 0-6-0 on goods at Billingborough. Fraser Ross

Graham Morfoot, who remained in the area up to closure remembered a J6 as the usual loco in the 50s, working the Grantham – Sleaford – Bourne turn, but after the closure of the northern section and the end of through trains, Ivatt 4MTs such as 43142 and J6 64268, working out of Spalding, served till the end of steam on the line.

4MT No 42532 at Neslam crossing. John Bonser

Billingborough train at Morton Rd September 1962 John Bonser

In its final days trains were worked by small Class O3 and O8 diesel locomotives again based at Spalding – D2025 and 7 were regular visitors – although a 4MT would usually be substituted to pull the heavier loads during the beet season.

Relics of the line

After closure, the lines, sleepers and any other equipment that had a scrap or resale value was lifted. Even the ballast was removed by locals like Pete Bristow.

"I remember carting the stone from the railway after the lines and sleepers had been removed with a Fordson Major with a front bucket on. We took this stone down Pointon Fen to re-stone our farm roadway."

The route of the line can be followed most of the way from Sleaford, which is still served by rail, to Bourne, although much of it is now in private ownership. Many of the station buildings are still standing, and a number of crossing houses also remain. Rippingale still has track in situ, and for some time housed the preserved 'Teddy Bear' shunter D9537 along with other rolling stock. A section of the line near Horbling, consisting of a cutting and an embankment is now a nature reserve. Access is from the site of the old 3-arch railway bridge on Stow Green Lane.

The bridge itself, the only large piece of engineering work on the line has been demolished, but not without some difficulty.

'It took three attempts, started with picks, shovels and pneumatic drills with little effect. Next was a wrecking ball on a crane, again with little effect. As a last resort explosives were used, it was a testament to the quality of build.' Graham Morfoot.

Aswarby and Scredington station used for wagon storage after closure. D Yarnell

Bibliography

Lincolnshire Railways, by Alan Stennett, Crowood Press 2016

Lost Railways of Lincolnshire, by Alan Stennett. Countryside Books 2007

Source Material of the Great Northern Railway, compiled by Guy Hemingway. GNRS 2000

The Great Northern Railway by John Wrottesley Vols 1-3 Batsford 1979

The History of the Great Northern Railway by Charles H Grinling 1898 Reprinted by George Allen & Unwin 1966

The Midland & Great Northern Joint Railway, by A J Wrottesley. David & Charles 1970

Bourne to Essendine, by John Rhodes. Pub KMS Books 1986.

Great Northern Branch Lines in Lincolnshire, by Stephen Walker. Pub KMS Books 1984.

The magazines of the Great Northern Railway Society, the Lincolnshire Wolds Railway Society, the Lincoln Railway Society and the Lincs and E Yorks Transport Review

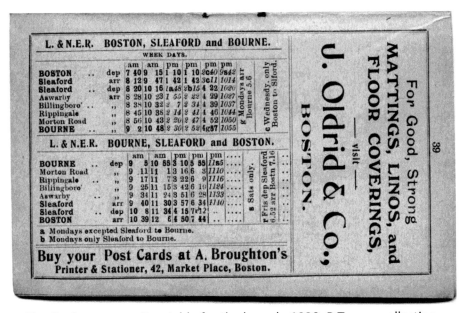

The final passenger timetable for the branch. 1930. R Tarpey collection